T0034809

JAMMIN' THROUGH THE SOUTH

KENTUCKY, VIRGINIA, TENNESSEE, MISSISSIPPI, LOUISIANA, TEXAS

DANIEL SEDDIQUI

SCHIFFER
PUBLISHING

4880 Lower Valley Road • Atglen, PA 19310

PREFACE

Connect with local experts. Learn their artistry. Understand something meaningful to the region. Craft a piece of history.

This travel guide is something special. You're not just visiting a place—rather, you are *being in* a place. Take it from me, your guide Daniel Seddiqui. I have been through the fifty states well over twenty times, and it never gets old. Engaging with new people, creating authentic experiences, and building newfound knowledge makes travel feel alive. From the start, I've envisioned a layout of the map (now Google Maps)—made of dots of cities and lines of highways—to become a reality, a life I call "Living the Map." My strategy of travel has always been to get to the heart of the people of a place and to learn how the natural environment inspires their innovation. From shooting archery with Cherokee Indians and building furniture with Amish craftsmen to cutting timber with Oregon lumberjacks, the memories I've made through experiential travel never fade and the relationships never dwindle, no matter how old I age.

To help bolster the meaning for travel and create a truly immersive experience, this book places a focus on Take It and Make It experiences. The Take It portion is about taking a lesson or joining in an activity, whether that is an instructed course or a leisurely pastime reflecting an area's local industry or culture. The Make It component is about handcrafting iconic symbols that the local artisans value, inspiring the traditional legacies and stories that we call America's craftsmanship. You'll learn new skills and have pieces of the region's pride to bring home with you.

Our immersive travel experience through the American South will focus on the region's extensive musical legacy. Enjoy your journey!

If you're more inclined to travel in a group, I lead organized tours. Visit www.livingthemap.com for more information.

—Daniel Seddiqui

CONTENTS

INTRODUCTION

The sounds of music are like a spirit of unearthed fog hovering over the cotton fields of the Mississippi delta, the rolling grass hills of Kentucky, the swampy bayous of Louisiana, the dense rural forests of Tennessee, and the brushlands throughout the plains of Texas. There's no doubting that the environment of the South inspired legendary musical artists to create America's most storied genres and songwriting. Authenticity is what keeps this music alive—hearing about the struggles and pain, the dreams and aspirations, and life as it was. America owns this music; influences come from its own backyard.

Traveling through the southern states, it's easy to imagine hearing twangling banjos and the vibrating harmonicas echoing the lands. Music is treasured as a way of life, whether going big in a Nashville parade or commemorating an impactful small-town artist at their birth home. This is where hometown musical heroes are on cities' welcome signs, and where the venues legends once played are preserved. Elvis Presley rocked the world to become the King of Rock and Roll from a rural town of Mississippi, and B.B. King revolutionized the way we hear the struggle from juke joints of Memphis. Getting her start singing in honky-tonks, Dolly Parton sang about a woman's perspective on romance.

Throughout this guide, you'll be learning about the history and development of southern-born genres, including ragtime, bluegrass, jazz, blues, country, gospel, rhythm and blues, Cajun, zydeco, and rock and roll. Pick up an instrument and play a tune on the grounds where legends once walked. Learn from those who practically live in the music studios to create the songs that will get crowds on their feet.

As they say, music is a soundtrack to your life. It's a time machine pulling on heartstrings of emotions. This tour of the South will take you places where music was inspired and still lives on today. Tour museums, drive iconic music highways, listen to live music, and take lessons from the best. You'll be jammin' through the South from Lexington, Kentucky, all the way to Austin, Texas.

CHAPTER 1

LEXINGTON, KENTUCKY

If there were an award for the city that most resembles an elaborate horse farm, Lexington would win it. Known as the Horse Capital of the World, Lexington borrowed central motifs of its large horse industry by installing the white vinyl fences commonly used on horse farms around its shopping centers, luxury communities, and parks. Also, as home to the University of Kentucky, this charming southern town is painted blue and white, decorated with the Wildcat pride of every resident. Kentucky's bluegrass

region is slow paced and harks back to times gone by, with customers patiently waiting in line as a client shares their life story with a bank teller, hand-laid stone walls lining scenic byways, and an Ale-8 with a moon pie serving as the go-to snack. Along with horses and the Wildcats, music is at the heart of the city—the blinding green tone of the region's pastures influencing the genre of music itself known as bluegrass.

CHECKING IN

Rose Hill Inn—*233 Rose Hill Avenue, Versailles*

You'll feel right at home—if your home resembles a stunning historic mansion in the countryside of Kentucky. Built in 1823 as the first structure along Rose Hill Avenue in historic downtown Versailles, this Victorian-style property has been revitalized by its owners for all to enjoy. The Rose Hill Inn is a step back in time, since much of the interior is original and the exterior has kept its Flemish-bond brickwork. The rooms are immaculate, and the grounds are meticulously groomed; you'll feel the tender love and care during your stay.

The grand fanned entrance of the Rose Hill Inn. *Courtesy of Rose Hill Inn / Robin Featheringill*

Gently rolling hills of the bluegrass region.
Courtesy of Visit Lexington / Mary Jane Speer

WHAT IS BLUEGRASS MUSIC AND WHERE DID IT GET ITS NAME?

It's safe to argue that "bluegrass" might be more associated with Kentucky than even Kentucky Fried Chicken. The term "bluegrass" has been applied to Kentucky's grass, a native genre of music, and even the state itself. But how did the lush ground cover of Kentucky's fields become associated with a style of music?

Kentucky is special enough to get a special name for its grass; the technical term is *Poa pratensis*. This type of meadow grass is used for livestock grazing and is believed to have been brought to the United States by early settlers. The seeds for bluegrass were a perfect choice for pioneers traveling during uncertain conditions, because the seeds can withstand harsh weather and grow especially well in the region's limestone soil. Although given the name "bluegrass," it is not actually blue but green; however, when fully grown, it does form blue flower heads. It is said to appear to have a blueish hue compared to

other grasses, and I've found this to be accurate in my personal experiences of driving through the Kentucky countryside. When taking in the views of these prairies, you'll notice something different about the grass.

Sandwiched between the Appalachian Mountains in the east and thick forests and waterscapes in the west, Kentucky's bluegrass region accounts for only one-fifth of the state's land, but this fertile pastureland in and around Lexington is what the state is known for. It was here in the 1940s that the style of music now known as bluegrass first took its name from local musician Bill Monroe's band: the Blue Grass Boys. The band's unique sound was further defined by the addition of Earl Scruggs and his three-finger picking style of banjo playing—a technique that gets listeners' toes tapping.

While even the International Bluegrass Music Association hasn't offered a conclusive definition on

what constitutes bluegrass music, its hallmarks include high-pitched, close harmonies (the "high lonesome sound") and dazzling instrumental play on acoustic guitar, mandolin, fiddle, upright bass, and five-string banjo played in Scruggs's three-finger picking style.

Family fun at the Southland Jamboree. *Courtesy of Southland Jamboree*

MAKE IT

Great Crossing Violins—*342 Viley Lane, Georgetown (roughly 30 minutes north of Versailles and Lexington)*
Don't come to a bluegrass jam empty-handed. Within the region, you can find musicians coming together to play and sing unrehearsed music, and in the bluegrass genre, instruments generally consist of the guitar, double bass, fiddle, five-string banjo, mandolin, steel guitar, and Dobro. Obviously, there's a heavy focus on string instruments. Whether you're an avid musician wanting to custom-make an instrument or just a music lover looking to secure a souvenir from the region, schedule an appointment to make your own violin at Great Crossing Violins with master craftsman Tommy Case at his workshop. It is not an established program, but Tommy allows visitors to learn his craft hands on, and assistants are always welcome.

What's a better gift from Kentucky than a handmade fiddle to reflect the state's iconic music genre of bluegrass? Of course, it takes months to handcraft a fiddle, but you can spend an hour or two learning about the process with a hands-on experience. The violin-making process starts with aged old-growth European figured maple, which is used for making the neck, scroll, sides, and back of the violin. The top of the violin is carved from aged tight-grain spruce. The raw wood for some of these violins is provided by a European tone wood supplier from Croatia. The next step is to glue two pieces of wood together; next, they get carved into Stradivari form with shaped ends and corner blocks. Learn how to bend ribs and insert fingerboards. Get a chance to chisel and scrape wood frames. Install the bass bar and neck. Pull some strings—and voilà! If you're hoping for a finished product, you can purchase a violin right inside the store. Schedule your session by calling 859-559-7341 or visiting www.greatcrossingsviolin.com.

INTERVIEW WITH CRAFTSMAN TOMMY CASE

What were your musical influences?

I was a listener of soul and rock and roll in the 1960–'70s, and then by the time I turned forty, I became more interested in traditional music. I was attending local outdoor festivals where family bands and bluegrass stars, like Ricky Skaggs, were accessible. I was enthralled by the mandolin and started to learn how to play on my own. When I was a little kid, I was interested in the fast paced fiddle tunes, and now that I'm older, I like instruments used for slower music.

How did you get started in crafting violins in particular?

In 2002, I worked in Frankfort, Kentucky, as a government official and had a friend that made cellos and violins. I enrolled into a two-year apprenticeship with him to learn how to handcraft violins.

End product of a six-quilted-front custom violin. *Courtesy of Tommy Case*

What are the main distinctions between string instruments?

Many instruments evolved from a lute. I'd say the scale length on a mandolin and violin are identical, but the mandolin has frets. It's easy to learn violin after the mandolin.

What kinds of musicians use your instruments?

I made pocket violins that Civil War reenactors use at historic sites in the area. For the bigger instruments, many come from the classically trained backgrounds that perform in the orchestras. I also make them for fiddlers like myself. I do love teaching young people how to make instruments, because it keeps the interest going with a pay-it-forward mindset. The apprenticeships now that I conduct and the future violins that my students will make expand my luthier expertise, and it will cultivate a new generation of central Kentucky luthiers that make and repair violins and other stringed instruments.

Best Venues to Listen to Bluegrass

It's not hard to find places to hear or play bluegrass in and around Lexington, so for your convenience here's a short list of venues suggested by locals and ranked by Visit Lexington. Pick a spot or two that best suits your curiosity and fits your schedule.

Red Barn Radio—*161 North Mill Street*
Bluegrass music is recorded live for Red Barn Radio, where audiences can listen to how broadcasting works. Red Barn Radio's mission is to promote and preserve the music of Kentucky. The musicians are accessible if you want to learn more about the music from locals and take pictures.

Southland Jamboree—*1152 Monarch Street*
Here's a perfect summer outing every Thursday, where you can experience music in the amphitheater and are encouraged to join the dance floor. It's an opportunity to listen to local artists and bluegrass headliners in a family-fun environment. The best part is that it's free.

University of Kentucky—*160 Patterson Drive*
Located at the Niles Gallery of the Lucille C. Little Fine Arts Library, the John Jacob Niles Center for American Music offers free noontime bluegrass concerts on Fridays. This series takes place every fall, so many students can gather and enjoy music on campus.

WoodSongs Old Time Radio Hour—*300 East Third Street*
On Monday evenings, the Lyric Theatre in downtown Lexington hosts national bluegrass acts in front of a live audience for radio. These music broadcasts are sent out to nearly five hundred media markets across the world.

Learn About the Best of the Best

Just an hour from Lexington, you can visit the **Kentucky Music Hall of Fame and Museum** at 2590 Richmond Street in Mt. Vernon. In 2002, the Museum and Hall of Fame introduced its first class of inductees and opened its doors. This is definitely a must-see attraction for music and history lovers. Built around the property's original riding stables, this museum aligns with the theme of horses, while the property hosts many local artists in the lobby and at the outdoor amphitheater with an authentic wooden stage. The museum is filled with memorabilia, artifacts, and exhibits that showcase not just bluegrass stars but Kentucky

artists of all musical genres. Last, make sure to interact with the musical instrument section to create your own tunes.

If you want to book an official concert at Kentucky's state-of-the-art music venue, check out the **Renfro Valley Entertainment Center** at 2380 Richmond Street, Mt. Vernon. Do you think they play bluegrass? Absolutely! And many other locally influenced musical genres can be heard as well. Make sure to check the concert listings at www.renfrovalley.com.

The Kentucky Museum and Hall of Fame, built on the site of former horse stables. *Courtesy of the Kentucky Music Hall of Fame*

⊚ WHILE YOU'RE HERE

You're here for the music, but you'd be remiss to visit Lexington without spending at least some time with the town's local celebrities—the thoroughbreds. Without watching a race at **Keeneland** at 4201 Versailles Road, a visit to Lexington is not complete. Many visitors and residents take trips to the Thoroughbred Center throughout the year to watch horses train for races at Keeneland in hopes of qualifying for the Kentucky Derby. Attendees' sundresses, blazers, and bowties are part of the Kentucky tradition at the races. There's a pre-party at the park, on a large, open grass field where guests sip on champagne and cocktails, and Keeneland hosts world-class races of competitors and guests from around the world. Just getting to hear the earth rumble as the horses pass makes the experience worth the trip. The auction house is also quite the spectacle; stop by to hear how much a yearling colt goes for—sometimes around $200,000. It's no wonder the Lexington area breeds not only horses but money. To get in the stirrups yourself, visit the **Kentucky Horse Park**, 4089 Iron Works Parkway. A guided thirty-five-minute trail ride, suitable for first-time riders, takes you along the outskirts of the park. When in Kentucky, do as the Kentuckians do.

A day at the races of Keeneland. *Courtesy of Visit Lexington / Mary Jane Speer*

CHAPTER 2

EASTERN KENTUCKY

Kentucky has two distinct sides of the state, with the Daniel Boone National Forest separating the luxurious horse farms, vast countryside roads, and urban cityscapes to the west from the rural unincorporated and underprivileged mountain towns to the east. The Appalachian Mountains are a special place, where culture runs deep generation after generation and the music is authentic as any you will find anywhere. There's not much outside

influence here, and the culture traces back to its Scotch-Irish heritage roots when the settlers found a remote part of the country when they arrived from Europe. Teenagers aren't rocking the latest American popular cultural trends here, instead preferring to stick to local traditions and proudly boosting the term "coal blooded." It's a place where time stands still, and that's beautiful.

CHECKING IN

Hampton Inn Pikeville—
831 Hambley Boulevard, Pikeville
Located 25 miles from Prestonsburg is a seven-floor, 123-room hotel in the heart of downtown Pikeville. Surrounded by businesses and cultural sites, visitors can enjoy being just a quick walk from Big Sandy Heritage Center, Appalachian Wireless Arena, Pikeville City Park, and Pikeville University. This hotel selection didn't just happen by accident; there are not many options of places to stay in rural Kentucky.

TAKE IT

US 23 Country Music Highway

The legendary names commemorated along Highway 23 make this a Road of Fame worth driving. During this Take It activity, you can take a drive where all the magic happened, and relive the musical influences stemming from this area, while also enjoying the unique landscape while traveling on serpentine-like roads through dense forest. It's so windy that hills must be blown by dynamite to make room. Eastern Kentucky is one of the most gorgeous landscapes imaginable—if you're able to see past a turn in the road. Overlooks are few and far between.

With this context in mind, it's extraordinary that music al artists from this part of the country have made a sound so loud that America knows their names. Lorretta Lynn, Chris Stapleton, Billy Ray Cyrus, the Judds, Ricky Skaggs, and Dwight Yoakam, to name a few, all hail from this area. Many of their songs are

Country Music Highway, cutting through hilly terrain of eastern Kentucky. *Courtesy of Paintsville Tourism*

based on life in the sticks or hollows. And did you know this region even has an instrument named after it? That's right—it's the Appalachian dulcimer, a three- or four-string instrument in the zither family that is played on the musician's lap and has a body the length of its fingerboard.

US 23 Country Music Highway Museum—*120 Stave Branch Road, Staffordsville*
Producing more country stars per capita than any other region, this eastern Kentucky city of Staffordsville is home to a museum with fourteen exhibits of memorabilia of locally born artists. The museum, which is located along Highway 23 from Ashland to Pikeville, also hosts performances by local musicians every Thursday at 7 p.m.

Butcher Holler, Home of Loretta Lynn—*Butcher Hollow Road, Van Lear*

To make it in this business, you either have to be first, great, or different. And I was the first to ever go into Nashville, singin' it like the women lived it. —Loretta Lynn

World famous for her song "Coal Miner's Daughter," Loretta Lynn sang with attitude and pride, bringing light to life in the holler to the rest of the world. Born Loretta Webb in 1932, she became the most-awarded country music artist of all time, earning the title "Queen of Country." She has sold forty-five million albums and has an amazing twenty-four No. 1 hits on the country music charts.

Detailed directions are necessary in eastern Kentucky, because cell phone reception and GPS signals are not guaranteed. From the intersection of Route 460/40/321 in Paintsville, take Route 321 south for 5 miles. Turn left on Route 1107 and travel 0.9 miles. Turn right on Route 302 for 1.5 miles and then turn left on Millers Creek Road. For tours, stop at Webb's General Store #5, on the right side of the road. Continue traveling Millers Creek Road, then turn left up Butcher Holler. The homeplace is located 2 miles past Webb's General Store.

Loretta Lynn's lyrics in her hit song "Coal Miner's Daughter" detail the pride of her upbringing, no matter how humble it may have been. The coal industry's company towns in Appalachia often provided only enough to families to just get by. Lynn expressed that although she and her family were poor, they still had love. The family cherished their father, who worked for the poor man's dollar in the nearby coal mines, while her mother took care of the children, did home chores until her fingers bled, and read the Bible by coal oil light. Loretta grew up with seven siblings, so you can imagine how tough it was to stretch a dollar on a miner's pay. Interestingly, many people in the region still face similar poverty today.

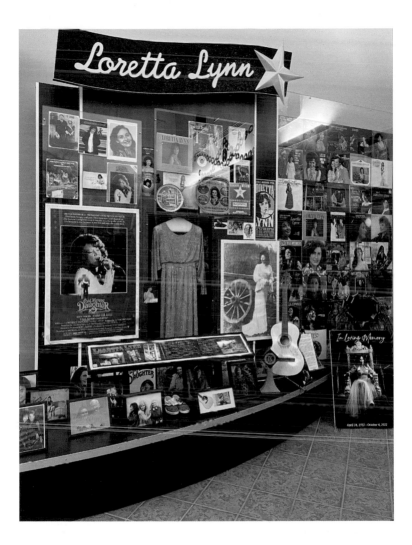

Country Music Highway Museum's exhibit of
Loretta Lynn. *Courtesy of Paintsville Tourism*

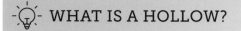

WHAT IS A HOLLOW?

The locals pronounce it "holler." This is a natural feature that makes eastern Kentucky and the Appalachian region distinctly unique. A hollow is a narrow valley between hills cut by a creek, where trailer homes and cabins reside on the sides of the creek. Typically, there's only one way to get in and out. This type of neighborhood is isolated, and it is heavily associated with extreme poverty because of a lack of opportunity and resources.

"Coal Miner's Daughter" represents the sentiment of the American can-do spirit. Coal mines had been operating in eastern Kentucky since 1820, and this song's release in 1970 gave voice to those who had been symbolically buried in the mines for more than a century.

Music in the Mountains

The Mountain Arts Center, 50 Hal Rogers Drive, Prestonsburg, is located within a stone's throw of US 23 Country Music Highway, which is certainly appropriate. This state-of-the art venue holds together the cultural fabric of eastern Kentucky's music, even while hosting national headlining acts. It's a huge space with a theater with more than one thousand seats, a commercial recording studio, and several arts education rooms for instructional music lessons. This site is rural! I'm talking right in a valley of mountain stone cut away to make room for the highway and the venue. This makes it even more impressive that many national headlining acts from a wide range of musical genres make their way here. And, of course, many of eastern Kentucky's favorite sons and daughters—such as

Loretta Lynn, Billy Ray Cyrus, Patty Loveless, Ricky Skaggs, Dwight Yoakam, and Chris Stapleton—have played here.

The Mountain Arts Center is also home to Billie Jean Osborne's Kentucky Opry and its Opry Junior Pros. If you want to watch a show that focuses on vocalists, then this would be the act. It showcases the pathway of promoting traditions of Appalachian music from one generation to the next, because young artists start from the age of six. The Mountain Arts Center welcomes volunteers, so if you want to volunteer as an usher or to help with stage setup, call the center's executive director at 606-886-2623 or visit macarts.com.

The one-thousand-seat theater at the Mountain Arts Center.
Courtesy of Joe Campbell

A studio soundboard at the Mountain Arts Center. *Courtesy of Joe Campbell*

TAKE IT

MAC's Arts Education Department provides individual instruction in piano, voice, violin/fiddle, guitar, banjo, mandolin, and visual arts, as well as group instruction in piano and voice. Although courses are typically a semester long, feel free to book a one-time session to feel and hear the delightful sounds. They do have a recording studio if you want to record your playing.

A unique experience would be booking a session with a vocal coach to teach you how to yodel. Although yodeling dates back thousands of years, to help farmers herd their flock of livestock, it has made its way into the musical scene, especially in Appalachia, which boasts its own peaks and valleys, just like in the Alps, where yodeling was a way of life. Singers incorporated lyrics and improvised harmonies that fit into music. It took centuries for yodeling to become a part of popular culture, but it did break through and can be found in *The Sound of Music's* "The Lonely Goatherd" song. Yodeling peaked in the 1940s and '50s, making it another Appalachian tradition that makes you feel like you are taking a step back in time. Call the Mountain Arts Center to inquire about booking a yodeling session. This new skill will surely impress your friends and family back home.

CHAPTER 3

BRISTOL, TENNESSEE/ VIRGINIA

Advertised as the mecca for music, Bristol is shared between two states, Virginia and Tennessee, which are split right down State Street; flags representing each state wave throughout downtown businesses. Bristol hosts some of the Southeast's largest events, such as NASCAR circuit races at Bristol Motor Speedway and a three-day festival called the Rhythm & Roots Reunion. Music brings a gathering in Bristol—or maybe a gathering

brings music in this historic mountain town, which is recognized as the Birthplace of Country Music.

Bristol doesn't get the attention it deserves, but it's a
humble town where stars get their humble beginnings.
Taking the drive through these hillscapes proves you have
to be intentional about making the stop, yet the experience
will be a reinvitation. It's hard not to feel welcomed by smiling
faces, comfort food, and a giant guitar statue for photo ops.

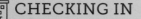

The Sessions Hotel—*833 State Street, Bristol, VA*

The area's authentic rural mountain appeal and nod to its music roots are heavily prominent in this repurposed historic complex, once used as a candy factory and mill. There's no shying away from the touches of music—from the massive outdoor lawn and performing stage for concerts to the Victrola radio, microphone lighting, and mega speaker lampshades. This seventy-room property is in the heart of the city, but there are plenty of excuses to stay on-site.

A touch of the music theme in the music guest room. *Courtesy of The Sessions Hotel*

Thousands of music lovers flock to Bristol for the annual Bristol Rhythm & Roots Reunion. *Courtesy of Charlene Baker*

Explore the Past and Present of Country Music

If you're coming to Bristol during the month of September, you're in luck. **Bristol Rhythm & Roots Reunion** music festival attracts thousands of regional and nonregional attendees to historic downtown Bristol for a three-day music extravaganza each September. The festival features the traditional sounds of Appalachia, where past meets present: up-and-coming stars shine, and local legends inspire. State Street, which splits Virginia from Tennessee, is where the crowds meet to eat, play, and engage with the traditional influences of music. It's an event that keeps the torch lit at the heart of the Birthplace of Country Music.

As much as people associate country music with Nashville, Bristol celebrates its own importance to the origins of the genre at the **Birthplace of Country Music Museum**, 101 Country Music Way Bristol, Virginia, which is one of the proudest museums affiliated with the Smithsonian Institution. The museum shares the story of how country music got its start with the 1927 Bristol Sessions—dubbed "the big bang" of country music by history scholars—which featured the first recordings of Jimmie Rodgers, known as the Father of Country Music, and the Carter family, the First Family of Country Music. The recordings launched the careers of these country legends and brought the genre to the masses, resulting in the US Congress's official designation of Bristol as the Birthplace of Country Music in 1998. The museum has become the epicenter for up-and-coming artists to engage with the roots of their music. It houses multiple theaters for concerts and community events, interactive displays, and educational programming.

Musicians perform at Bristol's musical extravaganza. *Courtesy of Charlene Baker*

TAKE IT

How do some of these local artists from a small town in the mountains of Tennessee manage to be heard by a much wider audience? The radio, of course. The Birthplace of Country Music Museum is even host to its own radio station, called Radio Bristol. In 2015, the

museum branched out to fund its own radio station through grants and donations. Inspired by the 1927 Bristol Sessions, Radio Bristol knew it would have an audience, and it is going strong worldwide today through streaming and the local radio station found on WBCM-LP, 100.1 FM. The station focuses on local and regional arts and culture, so a listener from Japan or Europe or anywhere else in the world can stream the station to learn about the integral part Bristol plays in the roots of American music through such shows as *Folk Yeah!*, *Dollar Country*, *Born in the Mountain*, and *Mountain Song and Story*. Visitors have an opportunity to take a lesson on how radio disc jockeys select songs and to discuss local topics regarding music with the station's hosts. Contact the Radio Bristol program director at 423-573-1927 to schedule a time with a selection of hosts.

A vintage stereo in the Birthplace of Country Music Museum's collection. *Courtesy of Charlene Baker*

MAKE IT

The Earnest Tube—*152 Lee Street Bristol, VA*
Whether you're a member of a jug band or a singing solo artist,
The Earnest Tube will turn your sounds into playable 12″ disc
recording, in the same way music was cut in the Bristol Sessions
of 1927, when "hillbilly" artists performing fiddle tunes, sacred
songs, string bands, and harmonica solos were commercially
viable. Step into this minimalist recording studio, just like the
Carter Family and Jimmie Rodgers. Book your session by calling
276-494-0141.

Above: Kris Truelsen in studio.
Courtesy of Charlene Baker

Opposite: Make the 1927 Bristol
Sessions your own. *Courtesy of
Discover Bristol / Briana Fillers*

RECORDING

⦿ WHILE YOU'RE HERE

NASCAR culture is heavily associated with the southern US region, originated by bootleggers that souped up their vehicles for weekend racing in the pastures. With drag racing, dirt track racing, and a part of the NASCAR series, the **Bristol Motor Speedway** at 151 Speedway Boulevard is a staple to the community. Even if you're not a fan of race cars, it may be worth the visit to meet the fans.

You'll discover that locals in the rural mountain communities like coming together to hang out outdoors. One of those popular outdoor events—which is still a thing today—is the **Twin-City Drive-In Theatre**. Park on the grass, bring a lawn chair, and enjoy screentime with a mountain backdrop at 2512 Volunteer Parkway.

CHAPTER 4

PIGEON FORGE, TENNESSEE

On the fringe of the Great Smoky Mountains National Park, this small-town escape of six thousand residents attracts more than nine million visitors a year. As the heart of the southeastern US, Pigeon Forge has grown to become a family-friendly Las Vegas in the mountains, inspired by Dolly Parton. That's right, this town's main attraction—which employs half the town—is Dollywood. Jam-packed with attractions, from outdoor adventures

and theme parks to dinner theaters and live music, Pigeon Forge is an accessible drive for southerners coming from Georgia, North Carolina, Alabama, and beyond—but make no mistake, visitors come from all over the world. There's something for everyone here, from outlet mall shopping to zip lines, and it's hard not to imagine hearing the delightful sound of Dolly's voice while you're enjoying it all.

🏨 CHECKING IN

Dollywood's DreamMore Resort and Spa—*2525 DreamMore Way*
If you're going to do Dollywood's theme parks, you might as well do it all with this Smoky Mountain resort that is just minutes away. Dolly Parton dreamed about sharing with the world her beloved life as a child in the great outdoors. She grew up in a one-room cabin in these mountains where a creaky old floor became her stage, and she has now proved what a nurturing imagination can create with this expansive wonderous property. Dollywood's DreamMore values the rich traditions of family and togetherness, just like Dolly does.

The resort's exterior. *Courtesy of the Pigeon Forge Department of Tourism*

Pigeon Forge. *Courtesy of the Pigeon Forge Department of Tourism*

WHO IS DOLLY PARTON?

Dolly Parton is recognized world-wide as a music legend, but her success story has humble roots. Growing up in Locust Ridge, Tennessee, in the Great Smoky Mountains, Parton was one of twelve children in a poor farming family. Her gift for singing was apparent at an early age, and she performed on local TV and radio programs as a child before moving to Nashville after completing high school.

Dolly Parton. *Courtesy of the Pigeon Forge Department of Tourism*

Parton became one of the bestselling female artists of all time, with twenty-five songs reaching the top of the country music charts. A prolific songwriter, Parton has composed thousands of songs, including "I Will Always Love You," "Jolene," "Coat of Many Colors," and "9 to 5." She has also received accolades for acting and writing.

Parton has been nominated for Emmy, Grammy, Oscar, and Tony awards and has been recognized for her contributions to music through the US Library of Congress Living Legend Award, Kennedy Center Honors, and the Grammy's Lifetime Achievement Award.

"My dream was to make as many people happy as I could in this life," Dolly has said, and she has become one of the most recognized and cherished popular figures in America.

Dolly's Tennessee Connections

Dolly Parton refers to her wonderous rural mountain roots often, including in one of her hit songs, "My Tennessee Mountain Home." She expresses that life was peaceful when she used to sit on her front porch listening to crickets in the summer and watching kids playing with June bugs on a string and chasing fireflies in the evening.

Dolly proves to be one of the great storytellers in music, since her wholesome lyrics resonate with rural America and bring perspective to those from less familiar environments. Song lyrics can often introduce listeners to a new language and regional vocabulary. For instance, those from the western United States will never encounter a firefly and might have never heard of this glowing insect. She sings about honeysuckle vine clinging to the fence along the lane. Again, many listeners may have never heard of honeysuckle, but it is abundant in the southern United States. It has a fragrance that makes the summer wind sweet.

My favorite part of the song is when Dolly mentions walking home from church on a Sunday with a loved one, talking about future plans and having genuine feelings about possibilities. Dolly paints a picture of the small-town slow pace— and a stroll like this can take place any day of the week, not just on Sundays. She created Dollywood to exemplify that possibilities start with an imagination. Her story of creating is an inspiring one that people can experience when visiting Pigeon Forge.

If you're inclined to learn more about Dolly Parton and her Tennessee roots, a new attraction called **The Dolly Parton Experience** is debuting in 2024. The former Chasing Rainbows Museum will offer an interactive, experiential approach to showcasing all things Dolly as visitors have the chance to view Dolly's family keepsakes, hear Dolly's story straight from Dolly herself, and much more.

The Chasing Rainbows Museum will give way to the new Dolly Parton Experience in 2024. *Courtesy of Pigcon Forge Department of Tourism*

MAKE IT

Old Flames Candles—*2700 Dollywood Parks Boulevard*
You might be thinking, "How is candle making related to music?" Well, long before musicians could play their instruments at home with electric power, they had candlelight. And, in the Great Smoky Mountains, this way of life lasted longer into modern day. Plus, you'll want to make a souvenir that relates to your visit to Dollywood. Who doesn't love the fragrance of candles and the romantic scenes they create? Meet with third-generation candle crafters to help shape and size your very own candle. This activity is possible for all ages and makes a great family affair.

⊙ WHILE YOU'RE HERE

There are countless family-friendly attractions in Pigeon Forge, including amusement parks, dinner theaters, and zip lines, but if you're looking to escape to the wildness, check out the **Great Smoky Mountains National Park**. From Pigeon Forge, it's just a thirty-minute drive to the entrance of the park. This southern national treasure is filled with stunning views, rushing rivers, and seemingly endless marked trails. The Smoky Mountains do have the effect of smoking mountains because the clouds often hover low into the dense trees. While driving the windy roads, sometimes into the thick clouds, it can make for a memorable visit.

CHAPTER 5

NASHVILLE, TENNESSEE

Nashville is evolving quicker than music, rewriting its song to blended genres and a new wave of transient culture. The city never loses its central tune though—after all, that's what attracts people to "Music City" in the first place: the artistry, showmanship, energy, and pride. Nashville has shown its value to the rest of the world and now has made a place on the stage for any-one to dance. Nashville is to musical artists as Los Angeles is to movie stars. There's no shortage of musical hotspots, where any site can be mistaken for a music video. The popular throughfare, Broadway, is the center

of musical action, saturated with honky-tonks, saloons, and bars. And visitors can get in on the fun too—learn how to line dance, holding your partner do-si-do. Pick up some leather cowboy boots and tap your heels for the two-step. There's a certain arrogance of the residents, knowing that their city is desirable and they get to live in it every day. It's no surprise that Nashville tops the list as one of the most prideful cities. As you walk around the city, you get the feeling that a hundred years from now, Nashville will still be celebrating its song, as the nation's music city.

MAKE IT

Delgado Guitars—*919 Gallatin Avenue #10*
Does your guitar have a story? Whether you are sitting around a fire, playing on stage for an open-mic night, or just displaying your instrument in the corner of your office, people love to hear the story of where you got your guitar. How about handcrafting one with Manuel of Delgado Guitars? Third-generation luthier (guitar maker) Manuel A. Delgado builds all the instruments sold in the store by hand and has built an impressive client list through the years. Guitars start as piles of wood. The backs and sides are usually made from sturdy hardwoods such as mahogany, rosewood, or maple. When lumber arrives at Delgado's guitar shop, it still contains some moisture from when the tree was alive. Before it can be cut into shapes, it has to be dried. This process happens over the course of months (or more than a year, in some cases) through a combination of sitting in climate-controlled storage and cooking in a kiln—a huge metal oven. Once it's dry, the wood is ready to be cut into the smaller pieces that compose a guitar's body, including the top, back, and sides (about 115 different parts go into each instrument!). Then the process continues with gluing, laser-cutting by a CNC machine, and design through

Manuel Delgado is a third-generation luthier. *Courtesy of Manuel Delgado*

INTERVIEW WITH CRAFTSMAN MANUEL DELGADO

For what genres of music do you feel the guitar is most significant?

The guitar is the central foundation to classical, country, mariachi, and so on, but I think blues or jazz would have less of a sound without the presence of the guitar.

How did you get involved with handcrafting?

I'm a third-generation guitar maker and fortunate enough to carry on the family business. I was bitten by the guitar bug at the early age of five years old. After years of playing, I realized I wasn't going to be the next megastar, because I found more passion behind lutherie. My craft is not about making guitars—rather, preserving the art of lutherie. We put something special into our work, and tradition and history matter more than mass production.

Has the music scene in Nashville grown, or has it always been this saturated?

[It has] expanded. People think of Nashville as only country music, but it's so much more. The city was first notably recognized by the Fisk Jubilee Singers. [*The Fisk Jubilee Singers are vocal artists and students at Fisk University, an HBCU in Nashville. The group performs shows around the world. The original Fisk Jubilee Singers introduced "slave songs" to the world in 1871 and were instrumental in preserving Negro spirituals, a unique American musical tradition.*] People around the world would suggest the singers must have come from a music city because of their brilliant performance. I would say the city of Nashville is coming back to its old roots by offering a multitude of genes, not just the six blocks of country music in downtown.

rosetting, bracing, side-bending, binding and pearling, sanding and filling, cutting the neck and fretboard, pleking, and, finally, stringing. Learn about many of these steps with Delgado by scheduling a one-on-one appointment by calling his shop at 615-227-4578.

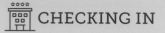

CHECKING IN

Gaylord Opryland Resort & Convention Center—
2800 Opryland Drive
Located in Music Valley, the resort allows guests to explore 9 acres of airy, indoor garden atriums with a beautiful lagoon and water channels navigated by gondolas. The restaurants and bars overlook the surrounding indoor views, making for a serene setting to enjoy a meal or drink. This is truly a unique experience, where you may feel like you're outside because of the vibrant tropical trees and flowers. The rooms are around the perimeter, and the location makes it very convenient to step over to the Grand Ole Opry to catch some of country music's most iconic concerts.

The resort's indoor garden atriums.
Courtesy of Visit Music City

Music, Music Everywhere

Show off your new guitar on **Broadway**, which is known as Honky Tonk Highway. Every day from 10 a.m. to 3 a.m., Nashville allows you to indulge in the gift of free music. Stroll the bustling sidewalks along with other pedestrians bouncing from one honky-tonk to another. Party trucks and tractors whiz by, blaring amplified music while passengers dance on the back beds. The flaring neon lights and vibrating sounds attract millions to explore Broadway. The bouncers stand by the doors, and the musicians are on stage right up against the windows, making for an accessible welcome inside. You may need to navigate around line dancers—or join in! If you don't know how to dance, visit the Wildhorse Saloon for a lesson.

Honky Tonk Highway. *Photo by Daniel Seddiqui*

Another music-centric spot to visit is **Music Row**, centered on Sixteenth and Seventeenth Avenues South. A musician's dream is to be signed by a record label, and there's a saturation of record companies along Music Row, including Foundry Records, River House Entertainment, and Warner Music Nashville. The neighborhood is considered the heart of Nashville's entertainment industry. Nestled within homes and buildings are the recording studios, from which some of your favorite songs came to be, including everything from Elvis Presley's "How Great Thou Art" (recorded at Historic RCA Studio B) to Foo Fighters' "Congregation" (recorded at Southern Ground Nashville). Take a short walk through these iconic quarters and read the plaques in front of the buildings to learn about the history of each studio.

Cleveland may have the Rock & Roll Hall of Fame, but Nashville is home to the **Country Music Hall of Fame and Museum** at 222 Rep. John Lewis Way South. Called "the Smithsonian to Country Music," this landmark preserves the history of country music while inspiring the next generation. Encompassing 350,000 square feet of exhibition galleries, archival storage, retail stores, and event space, this is a spectacular site to feed your love for country music. If you're a fan of Alabama, Ray Charles, Gene Autry, Brooks and Dunn, George Strait, and many others, this is the place to get close to their legacy.

A music studio in Nashville. *Photo by Daniel Seddiqui*

Nashville's Music Row. *Courtesy of Larry Darling*

◉ WHILE YOU'RE HERE

Considering that Music Row is just blocks from the bustling college district of Midtown, be sure to explore Vanderbilt University's campus—and **the Parthenon**. That's right, the Parthenon. Located in Nashville's Centennial Park, this structure is the world's only exact-size and detailed replica of the original temple in Athens, Greece. While it may seem strange to have a celebration of the epitome of Greek classical architecture in the American South, the replica was built when Tennessee celebrated its one hundredth year of statehood with the Tennessee Centennial Exposition—as an homage to Nashville's nickname "Athens of the South."

A few blocks down, a new museum called the **National Museum of African American Music** opened in 2021 at 510 Broadway. It's the only museum of its kind dedicated to preserving and celebrating the history of Black music in America. Visitors can learn about more than fifty musical genres through a variety of artifacts and interactive technology.

Best Venues to Listen to Country

Ryman Auditorium—*116 Fifth Avenue North*
Coldplay calls it the "greatest theatre in the world." They're not alone in this belief, since many of music's headliners agree. Originally built in 1892 as the Union Gospel Tabernacle, the legendary venue was the previous home to the Grand Ole Opry. History is made at the Ryman like a revolving door. Some of music's most defining moments of all genres happened here: Hank Williams's six encores, Johnny Cash falling in love with June Carter, and Patsy Cline's Opry debut. Today, it is rated the top site to visit in Nashville—and not just of the music venues but of any site.

Bluebird Cafe—*4104 Hillsboro Pike*
It seats only ninety, but this preeminent listening room has gained world fame as the city's incubator of talent. Taylor Swift is just

one of many artists discovered there. The locals appreciate this low-key venue far from the showy honky-tonks of Broadway. Over 70,000 visitors come through the doors annually, and celebrity appearances are common.

Grand Ole Opry House—*2804 Opryland Drive*
The Opry remains the platform that connects country artists and fans to the music they love. Just about every country artist has performed there, and it is a must-see stop while in Nashville. This is the stage that showcases generations of music and has put country music on the map. Performing at the Grand Ole Opry is a major achievement for any musician—almost akin to becoming an instant hall of famer. Today, the venue hosts the nation's oldest live music broadcasts, which can be heard through streaming or on 650 AM radio.

The Station Inn—*402 12th Avenue South*
If you enjoy intimate venues where you can circle around the fiddle, banjo, and mandolin players, this spot will offer your most memorable spectator experience in Nashville. Bluegrass, American roots, and classic country are played seven nights a week. If you hear people refer to "the Gulch" between downtown and music row, the Station Inn is in the heart of it.

Robert's Western World—*416-B Broadway*
Some might say this venue is the staple of Lower Broadway. You'll see the crowds coming and going through the doors until 3 a.m. The old-country-style theme and the music keep this site appealing to generations. The venue even kicks off Sunday mornings with traditional gospel.

The Troubadour—*2416 Music Valley Drive*
If you want to enjoy music in a theater, head to this site, which has been hosting radio broadcasts since 1947. The venue hosts

a cowboy church and traditional country artists. It's always a fantastic place to make friends.

American Legion Post 82—*3204 Gallatin Pike*
This East Nashville gem hosts weekly shows, which include classic country, western, and hillbilly bands. Dance lessons are included if you want to square-dance or contra dance.

TAKE IT

Wildhorse Saloon—*120 Second Avenue North*
There's no more friendly and fun place to learn how to line-dance than Wildhorse Saloon, located only a half block from Broadway. This 66,000-square-foot restaurant, club, and live concert venue is filled with history. Over 1.5 million guests stop by every year to watch the likes of Darius Rucker, Lady Antebellum, Rascal Flatts, Ringo Starr, Etta James, Pat Benatar, Rick Springfield, and Gladys Knight—to name just a few stars who have graced the venue's stage. Some argue that the venue's main attraction is its oversized dance floor, where you can learn how to line-dance. As a participant in the past, I agree this was the most fun and inviting—and, most importantly, embarrassment-free—scene to dance. There are so many dancers, nobody will even notice if you miss a step.

No reservations are needed to join the dance floor! With decades of experience, their great instructors can tailor dances to any age and ability, and you'll be guaranteed to have a smile on your face—even when you're dealing with the frustration of your feet. The dance floor is fully open, and they welcome dancing at any time, including during the band sets. At Wildhorse Saloon, they don't walk the line, they dance it!

Wildhorse Saloon. *Photo by Daniel Seddiqui*

WHAT'S THE DIFFERENCE BETWEEN LINE DANCING AND SQUARE DANCING?

Line dancing involves set choreography for which most participants already know the moves, and it is performed to familiar songs. Square dancing is much different, using a "caller" who tells the dancers what moves to do next, Simon Says style. Square dancing is often done without vocals to noncommercial or underground songs. While both of these dance styles are often associated with country music today, they have roots in music of a different kind; both evolved from the 1600s in Europe.

MAKE IT

Nashville Picks

Guitar picks can be a simple and small souvenir of Nashville, and Dustin Headrick makes picks from currency and precious metals. He makes many of his picks at his home studio and in front of festivalgoers around town, but you can also book a hands-on experience with him in Nashville. The techniques used to craft these guitar picks are marvelous but can also be tedious. Schedule an appointment to shave and polish your own US quarter coin guitar pick by sending Dustin an email at nashvillepicks@gmail.com. Dustin can meet you anywhere in town.

A quarter becomes a guitar pick.
Courtesy of Dustin Headrick

INTERVIEW WITH CRAFTSMAN DUSTIN HEADRICK

How do you make some of your illustrious picks?

I start with the raw material. Whether it's stone, natural soft materials, or metal, whatever; I'm up to experiment with any material just to see what it sounds like! Next I hand-shape the pick based on the style of pick I want to create. Often the material tells me what shape it wants to be. I will use either a handsaw, jigsaw, hand shear, scroll saw, or rotary wheel to find that shape. Then I bevel the edges based on the pick design; that's typically done by hand, using a file with varying grits or with specialty rotary wheels. Then comes the fine-tuning; this is where it gets tricky—it's the prepolish and finishing of the edges, which is the most important part. Every pick is inspected to make sure there are no flaws that will impede the final polishing process. If there's a flaw at this point, then the entire process

TAKE IT

has to begin again. At last [it's time for] the final polishing. Metal picks are hand-polished using various rotary wheels and jewelry compound; natural materials have their own various compounds, wheels, and hand-polishing techniques, and some materials like stone spend days (or weeks!) in a tumbling process. At the end of it all, I have a stunningly handcrafted guitar pick that I can use to make beautiful music—and hopefully inspire other artists to do the same!

Interstate 40 (Music Highway) Even when you're on your way out of town, Nashville provides another way to experience music. Marked with music notes for 222 miles along Interstate 40, this stretch of highway celebrates musical accomplishments from Nashville (Music City) to Memphis (the Birthplace of Rock and Roll and the Home of the Blues). It's claimed to be the most influential music geographical location in the world, and there are plenty of worthwhile stops along the way.

Hurricane Mills

Take a tour of the **Loretta Lynn Dude Ranch**, 8000 Highway 13 South, which was Loretta Lynn's permanent residence. This stunning property hosts tons of attractions and entertainment.

Camden

The Patsy Cline Memorial at 2082 Mount Carmel Road is the site of the tragic plane crash that claimed the lives of country singers Patsy Cline, Cowboy Copas, and Hawkshaw Hawkins and pilot Randy Hughes on March 5, 1963.

Henderson

Henderson is the birthplace of country music singer Eddy Arnold, and members of Kings of Leon, a rock band that formed in Nashville, also have ties to the town.

Jackson

In Jackson, you'll find the **home of Carl Perkins** at 2263 North Highland Avenue. Known for "Blue Suede Shoes" and other hits, Perkins left a musical legacy through his pioneering of rock and roll. Paul McCartney once even said, "There would have been no Beatles, if it were not for Carl Perkins."

Another spot to check out in Jackson is the **International Rock-A-Billy Hall of Fame** at 105 North Church Street. Commemorating rockabilly, an early stage in the evolution of rock and roll, the site features pictures and memorabilia of rockabilly artists and an outdoor pavilion. Dance halls were packed in the early 1950s, and this site still welcomes live performances.

Jackson has other important musical ties as well. Hard Rock Cafe and House of Blues cofounder Isaac Tigrett opened his first Hard Rock Cafe in America at the Old Hickory Mall in Jackson. The town is also the birthplace of Sonny Boy Williamson, the Father of the Modern Blues Harp, who toured with such legendary greats as Muddy Waters, Yank Rachell, and Sleepy John Estes. Williamson is credited with being the first artist to utilize the harmonica as a lead instrument.

Brownsville

Visitors can check out the **Tina Turner Museum**, which is located at 121 Sunny Hill Cove in a former one-room, Blacks-only schoolhouse once attended by Turner. In tribute to Turner, who has won twelve Grammys, sold more than 100 million albums, and is referred to as the Queen of Rock and Roll, the building showcases her flashy outfits, platinum and gold albums, and tons of pictures.

Located on the same grounds is the last home of Sleepy John Estes, a world-famous "bluesman" who influenced the likes of Robert Plant and Bob Dylan with his legendary style and career spanning six decades.

CHAPTER 6

MEMPHIS, TENNESSEE

Memphis has played a significant role in forming America's identity, and this iconic city has an obligation to preserve its history like exhibits in a museum. Voices have proven to be amplified here, as seen in the evolving music sounds of Elvis Presley, Johnny Cash, and B.B. King. And while the assassination of Martin Luther King Jr. in Memphis silenced one of the great voices of his time, the devastating loss also spurred the spread of his message of justice and equality to the ends of the earth.

Remnants of the past will always remain present because the light that Memphis has created is too significant to bury. The proof is in the lyrics, since Memphis is mentioned in more than a thousand songs, a total that the visitors bureau proudly boasts is more than any other city in the world. The downtown trolley train's bell is ringing, the Mississippi River bridge's lights are flashing, and the voices of Memphis are still heard from one generation to the next.

CHECKING IN

Hotel Napoleon—*179 Madison Avenue* Located in downtown Memphis's historic Winchester building and listed on the National Register of Historic Places, this elegant hotel dates back to 1902. Built by Napoleon Hill, tagged as the merchant prince of Memphis, the hotel is a staple within the neighborhood, which includes other famous landmarks such as FedExForum and lively Beale Street. There's a lot within walking distance to make your stay even more entertaining. The staff is very accommodating, the rooms are spacious with great lighting, and the classic architecture of the lobby will have you appreciated local craftsmanship.

Hotel Napoleon. *Courtesy of Memphis Travel*

MAKE IT

Metal Museum—*374 Metal Museum Drive*

Walking down the iconic Beale Street, you'll find brass music notes on the sidewalk, similar to the stars on the Hollywood Walk of Fame. Also notice the music notes on patio railings, neon signs, and various other places. You can even create your own version of this common Memphis motif by learning how to cast a music note ornament from metal. This molten material is poured into a mold cavity, which takes the form of the finished part. The molten material then cools, with heat generally being extracted via the mold, until it solidifies into the desired shape. The only one of its kind in North America, the Metal Museum exhibits artists' metalwork and offers public programs, including

Beale Street. *Photo by Daniel Seddiqui*

the one where guests can make their very own music note ornament. The manicured grounds, complete with a beautiful sculpture garden, look like they could be the site of an elegant storybook wedding. Plus, the views of the Mississippi River are the best of anywhere in the city. Book an appointment four to six weeks in advance at metalmuseum.org.

Step into Music History

After creating a Memphis memento, continue making music-related memories at two iconic local museums. Visit **Sun Studio** at 706 Union Avenue to learn why Memphis is recognized

Making metal music notes.
Courtesy of Houston Cofield

Before leaving Memphis, visit the **National Civil Rights Museum** at 450 Mulberry Street, the site of the Lorraine Motel, where Martin Luther King Jr. was assassinated. Learn about how King left his legacy for those fighting for justice and freedom and be inspired by one man's purpose and the sacrifices he made for a better today.

Also, take the pedestrian bridge or Memphis monorail to **Mud Island**, a small peninsula in the Mississippi River that captures the greatest view of the Memphis downtown skyline. In the evenings, the bridges along the river put on a dazzling light show.

The Lorraine Motel. *Courtesy of Travel Memphis*

worldwide as "the Birthplace of Rock and Roll." This storied spot is the location of the discovery of such musical legends as B.B. King, Elvis Presley, Johnny Cash, and Jerry Lee Lewis, as well as an incubator in the 1950s of musical genres from blues and gospel to country and rock and roll. Tour guides share inside stories of B.B. King, Howlin' Wolf, Ike Turner, Elvis, Johnny Cash, Carl Perkins, Jerry Lee Lewis, and Roy Orbison, and visitors can even see the spot where Elvis first approached the secretary's desk and asked to audition and make his first recording.

Just as iconic is **Stax Studio**, 926 East McLemore Avenue, where the focus is soul music. You won't believe how many hits came out of this studio; it's the reason why Memphis is also known as "Soulsville." There are many amazing exhibits and memorabilia from the biggest stars of soul, gospel, funk, and blues, and you can enjoy a self-guided tour through one of the best music museums in the country.

Best Places to Hear the Blues

After a day learning about local music history, go hear the sounds of the city for yourself live on Beale Street. You'll have a new appreciation for the performing artists who are keeping the sounds of yesterday alive while implementing their own new twist. The neon signs create a vintage appeal to Beale Street, which is considered one of the iconic streets of America, along with the Las Vegas Strip and Broadway of Nashville.

B.B. King's Blues Club—*143 Beale Street*

You can spot the sign a mile away, making this spot one of the most popular in Memphis. Home to live entertainment every night of the week, the club dishes out not just authentic blues,

Stax Studio now houses exhibits and memorabilia. *Courtesy of Ronnie Booze*

classic soul, and rock and roll but also some of the South's iconic menu items. Memphis is synonymous with barbecue, so get your fill for music and award-winning ribs in a one-joint stop for lunch, dinner, or a late-night meal.

Rum Boogie Cafe—*182 Beale Street*
Established in the midst of the 1980s renaissance of Memphis's entertainment district, Rum Boogie Cafe is stealing a lot of attention on Beale Street. Its "Down Home Cookin', Down Home Blues" motto appeals to those looking for a noncommercial, modest southern experience. Every night of the week, you can enjoy music, including blues, country, gospel, and rock and roll.

Wild Bill's Juke Joint—*1580 Vollintine Avenue*
A juke joint is an informal establishment of music, dancing, gambling, and drinking, most commonly associated with African Americans of the South. If you're looking for one located outside Beale Street, this is the spot. Wild Bill's is home to a museum and keeps its traditions rooted for the community.

Silky O'Sullivan's—*183 Beale Street*
With an inviting atmosphere for casual dining with family and friends, this spot features a menu that ranges from great barbecue and ribs to fresh oysters on the half shell, as well as live blues music. Don't miss the nightly dueling pianos.

WHERE WAS THE BIRTHPLACE OF ROCK AND ROLL?

Some claim rock and roll was born in Cleveland; others say New Jersey. Memphis is a possibility. Hattiesburg, Mississippi, is another one. The debate will live on, but the strongest clue to the genre's origin is that it is derived from rhythm-and-blues music of the 1940s. Rock and roll also has hints of gospel, country, and folk music, and it's influenced by boogie-woogie, up-tempo jazz, and swing. During the next few decades that followed the 1940s, such stars as Chuck Berry, Fats Domino, and Elvis Presley emerged; the common theme is they were all from along the southern portion of the Mississippi River, but Memphis is where much of the collaboration of artists took place.

Memphis vs. Cleveland

There's an ongoing debate about which city has a better claim to the "Birthplace of Rock and Roll" title. Cleveland's stake is largely based on the efforts in the 1950s of radio personality Alan Freed and record store owner Leo Mintz, both of whom were early champions of an emerging style of popular music that they dubbed "rock and roll," borrowing a term from blues. Freed is credited with staging the first-ever rock-and-roll show, the Moondog Coronation Ball, in Cleveland. Thanks to the efforts of FM radio station WMMS in the 1970s and 1980s, Cleveland maintained its importance in the rock-and-roll scene. Its importance to the genre was cemented when the Rock & Roll Hall of Fame Foundation decided that Cleveland would be the site of its museum, which opened in 1995.

But Memphis also has a strong claim as the Birthplace of Rock and Roll: Jackie Brenston and his Delta Cats recorded "Rocket 88," considered to be the first-ever rock-and-roll single, at Memphis's Sun Studio.

Opposite: Graceland's record wall.
Courtesy of Elvis Presley's Graceland

The Home of the King

You can't go on a music tour of the South without fully engaging with the legacy of Elvis Presley, the King of Rock and Roll, by visiting **Graceland** at 3764 Elvis Presley Boulevard. Over a half-million people per year visit Graceland, the iconic property of Elvis and his family. At the age of twenty-two, Elvis purchased this mansion. Across the street is **Elvis Presley's Memphis**, which hosts an astounding collection of his memorabilia and accolades. A 40-foot wall showcases just some of the achievements of his hit records. The entirety of Graceland's property takes up a full city block, and it's filled with shops and restaurants. Elvis has sold more than one billion records, and this site showcases 1.5 million artifacts relating to him, even including planes and cars. With so many documented accomplishments, you would think Elvis lived for two hundred years rather than only forty two, but Graceland shows that his legacy lives on after his death.

Elvis's iconic home. *Courtesy of Elvis Presley's Graceland*

CHAPTER 7

MISSISSIPPI DELTA

Mississippi at one time was the wealthiest state of the Confederacy because of the booming cotton industry. The delta was the heart of it all. During the early 1900s and after the abolishment of slavery, millions of southerners fled to escape the oppression of Jim Crow, which were segregation and disenfranchisement laws of the South that often spawned racial violence and economic and educational oppression. Cities such as Chicago and Detroit were major destinations in a movement called the Great Migration. The cotton industry fell apart, and many of those who stayed in the region suffered financially and lacked opportunity. Today, the Mississippi delta is one of the poorest

places in America and suffers from scars of the past, but it's authentic and filled with character. People are genuinely kind, making for another reason to visit this distinct region.

The Mississippi delta is known as the Birthplace of the Blues and has been referred to as the "cradle of American civilization." Defined by the Oxford dictionary as "melancholic music of black American folk origin, typically in a twelve-bar sequence," blues music reverberated around the world and led to the birth of jazz, country, rhythm and blues, and—of course—rock and roll. All these genres were inspired by the struggles of those working the cotton fields of the Mississippi delta.

TAKE IT

Mississippi Blues Trail—*US Highway 61*

Journey along US Highway 61, America's Blues Highway, discovering the roots of American music. This unique stretch along the Mississippi River from Tunica to Natchez is like no other. Although it is an excruciatingly impoverished region of the country, where it sometimes feels like the modern world has ceased to exist, the Mississippi delta and its blanketed white fields of cotton, barbecue shacks, and abundance of rural churches are the iconic sites of the Deep South. This is the Mississippi delta, where blues is a culture and a way of life that touches everyone.

The roots of blues music can be found in the Mississippi delta. *Courtesy of Tunica Convention & Visitors Bureau*

The Mississippi Blues Trail celebrates the enormous achievements of famous blues musicians throughout the state, including Muddy Waters, B.B. King, and Robert Johnson. Historical markers are scattered throughout the region to spotlight important sites, whether at the birthplace of a musical legend, juke joints where magic happened, or a museum with precious artifacts and memorabilia. There are over two hundred interpretive markers in Mississippi, but the delta region has the highest concentration of blues history.

WHAT IS THE MISSISSIPPI DELTA?

The Mississippi delta is a giant plain of some of the most fertile soil in the world, comprising nearly 7,000 square miles mostly in Mississippi. The land is the old floodplain of the Yazoo and the Mississippi Rivers and is now protected by levee and reservoir systems. With this unique natural feature developed a rich history and culture to go with it. The delta is also known for catfish—and locals often catch fish with their bare hands, called noodling.

MAKE IT

Gateway to the Blues Museum—*13625 Highway 61 North, Tunica Resorts*
Right off Highway 61 sits the Gateway to the Blues Museum, which is the perfect entry to the Mississippi Blues Trail. A must-see attraction for all music lovers, the museum tells the remarkable story of how the blues was born and the role Tunica played in building the genre's legacy. Learn about the history of the blues by engaging with the museum's exhibits and artwork in galleries highlighting "What Is Blues?," "Why the Mississippi Delta?," "Evolution of Style and Form," "Mississippi Bluesmen," and

"Evolution of the Guitar." Nothing beats the recording studio, where you can learn the basics of blues music and even record your own song. In an interactive exhibit in the Blues Lyric Interactive gallery, local bluesman Memphis Jones will teach you AAB blues songwriting style and allow you to record your very own blues song. Once you are done with your song, it can be made available via email so that you can keep it as a one-of-a-kind memento of your time in the delta.

Above: The Gateway to the Blues Museum, located off Highway 61. *Courtesy of Tunica Convention & Visitors Bureau*

Left: Museum visitors can record their own blues song. *Courtesy of Tunica Convention & Visitors Bureau*

Clarksdale, Mississippi

Call it a humbling city, where it feels like a visit is a few decades late. The main attraction is music, and that still brings in a constant flow of visitors to listen to the stories of the past through the soothing sounds of the saxophone and bass voices on the microphone. One of the larger cities of the delta, Clarksdale is saturated with music joints and stages in just about every place of business. The paint has worn off the vacant buildings and crumbled pavement of the lots, but the authenticity still shines.

Listen to live music at **Ground Zero Blues** at 387 Delta Avenue. Co-owned by actor Morgan Freeman, the venue welcomes patrons to listen to the music of the "real deal" local artists who keep the sounds of their forefathers alive. Take a visit to **Red's Lounge** at 398 Sunflower Avenue for a hole-in-the-wall setting, where music is the only attraction. Clarksdale is also home to the **Delta Blues Museum**, a place where visitors find meaning, value, and perspective by exploring the history and heritage of the blues. You can't leave Clarksdale without learning a tune or two.

TAKE IT

Deak's Mississippi Saxophone & Blues Emporium—
13 Third Street
Take a harmonica lesson from Deak Harp himself. A national blues icon, Deak felt the power of blues from his home in New York, when he decided to relocate to Mississippi and dedicated his life to his music. "We all have pain," he explained. "I didn't have to pick cotton during the civil rights era for blues music to

speak to me and heal my sorrow." You'll never meet a more passionate individual, and he's open to discussing his love for the harmonica. He'll jam out in his store for an impromptu audience, and you'll never know when he'll stop. Could be five minutes. Could be an hour. You're in for a treat, no matter how long he plays. He's a great example of feeling the vibe of the blues and getting into the zone.

Above: Deak Harp jams out in his store.

Cleveland, Mississippi

Head for Cleveland, Mississippi, to explore **Dockery Farms** at 229 Highway 8, where the blues began. Music legends such as B.B. King refer to Dockery Farms as the exact birthplace of blues. Scholars and fans agree that the site of a historic plantation community in the heart of the Mississippi delta was pivotal in the development and widespread attraction of the genre. In 1895, Will Dockery established this 26,000-acre plantation to produce cotton, which was the nation's most important export in the nineteenth and early twentieth centuries. For the African Americans who picked cotton, the arduous work created a culture that inspired the music. Singing was a way of expressing pain and making the time go faster.

Cleveland is now home to the **GRAMMY Museum** at 800 West Sunflower Road. The museum features award-winning stars and focuses on Mississippi-born musicians such as Faith Hill and 3 Doors Down. There are many workshops offered that feature some of the industry's latest technology. It's one of the busiest museums in the state.

The B.B. King Museum. *Courtesy of Robert Terrell*

Just a few miles away, complete the Mississippi Blues Trail at the Indianola birthplace of the legendary B.B. King. Visit the **B.B. King Museum** at 400 Second Street to learn about his childhood and how he became one of the blues genre's greatest pioneers.

Natchez, Mississippi

Called the "Little Easy," Natchez is considered the birthplace of Mississippi, with rich heritage shaped by Africans, French, British, and Spaniards. This quaint southern town draws in droves of visitors who indulge in viewing the old-style architecture of the antebellum homes. Natchez was first settled by the French as a fort on a bluff overlooking the Mississippi River, but the Natchez Indians first inhabited the area. In the late 1700s, the French and Indians brought slaves of the Bambara tribe from Africa, making them the first slaves in the state. With these blended cultures, it's no wonder Natchez is such a manmade wonder. Today, you can enjoy not only the architecture, but also the **Natchez Trace Parkway**, which allows travelers to explore 10,000 years of history on a 444-mile recreational road and scenic drive through three states that starts here. It roughly

A tour highlighting Natchez's antebellum architecture. *Courtesy of Visit Natchez*

follows the "Old Natchez Trace," a historic travel corridor used by American Indians, "Kaintucks" (frontiersmen), European settlers, slave traders, soldiers, and future presidents. Today, people can enjoy not only a scenic drive but also hiking, biking, horseback riding, and camping along the parkway.

Natchez is proudly a part of the **Gold Record Road**, which shares the space within a triangle shaped by Nashville, Memphis, and New Orleans. The road loops twice through Natchez, where Mississippi Blues Trail markers and music venues can be found. The city is home to several juke joints, restaurants, and bars that offer music each night.

Built in the late 1700s or early 1800s, the **Under the Hill Saloon** at 25 Silver Street is one of the most historic spots on the Mississippi River. Once a stopping point for "thieves, cut-throats, ladies-of-the-night and riverboat gamblers," the saloon now features live music every weekend and is a popular gathering spot for Cajun music and strong drinks.

⌂ CHECKING IN

Dunleith Historic Inn—
84 Homochitto Street, Natchez
Built in 1855, this pre–Civil War mansion, nestled among large Mississippi oak trees and encompassed by a wrought-iron fence, offers an experience of authentic southern hospitality. Dunleith Historic Inn is a national historic landmark and is a prime example of antebellum architecture.

Dunleith sits on a 40-acre estate, which includes an original 1790s carriage house, a dairy barn, a poultry house, a greenhouse, and a three-story brick dependency. The main mansion has a Greek Revival design and includes twenty-six Tuscan columns built of brick and stucco. Porches surround the entire building on the first and second floors.

The hotel's grand exterior.
Courtesy of Dunleith Historic Inn

CHAPTER 8

NEW ORLEANS, LOUISIANA

The Big Easy is an escape from reality, like being on a Monopoly board of the classically recognized streets, such as St. Charles Avenue, Magazine Street, Bourbon Street, Canal Street, Royal Street, and Audubon Place. New Orleans is a true gem of America, yet ironically it's one of the few cities that doesn't fit the "typical" American city. The city of New Orleans is exotic and defined by the extraordinary—this is not the everyday music you'd

hear, food you'd try, architecture you'd see, or nature you'd encounter elsewhere. New Orleans was ahead of its time, blending a cultural melting pot into its own authentic identity, finding its groove after centuries of molding. The bustling energy of New Orleans is incomparable, and that's the shrimp and grits to make this a global hotspot for tourism.

Exploring the Big Easy

Soak up jazz in the very city where jazz was born at the **New Orleans Jazz Museum** at 400 Esplanade Avenue. The museum teaches visitors about jazz and all its forms through exhibitions, educational opportunities, and an array of live performances and concerts. Check the calendar for concerts and festivals.

Just a few blocks away is the popular **Jackson Square**—and there's no other way to describe it other than referring to it as magical. It's the backdrop of the St. Louis Cathedral, and if you

🏨 CHECKING IN

Bourbon Orleans Hotel—*717 Orleans Street*

The Bourbon Orleans Hotel is in the heart of the city, central to downtown and in proximity to the French Quarter. Just as if you're in Paris, you'll be inspired to walk anywhere from your room to explore the neighborhood's many attractions. The rooms are gracious in hospitality—elegant and inviting. Locals know this iconic and historic landmark, and it's clear that the establishment's reputation matters to those who work to deliver the best stay possible.

Bourbon Orleans Hotel. *Courtesy of Ashley McCain*

are there to catch a colorful sunset, it looks like a masterpiece painting. Most people don't realize that this gem is right on the Mississippi River. It's so easy to get lost in the French Quarter with all the excitement, music, and shops, but there's a serious natural feature just a block away. If you want to experience quint-essential New Orleans, eat on the balcony of Tableau overlooking Jackson Square and listen to local performers while tasting the fine cuisine. The free music around these quarters is jubilant to say the least. The trombone might be the main attraction, since it's a rare find in bands.

Afterward, take a stroll through **Louis Armstrong Park** to capture some images of statues depicting the legendary jazz artist, as well as many other sculptures depicting other subjects.

Louis Armstrong Park. *Courtesy of Paul Broussard*

☀ WHO WAS LOUIS ARMSTRONG?

An artist who will live on forever, Louis Armstrong has been an influential figure not only in the recording studio but also in films, on radio, and on television. His iconic hit "What a Wonderful World" wasn't even a chart-topper until after his passing, proving that his legacy stands the test of time. It is safe to say that his recordings with his innovative bands the Hot Five and the Hot Seven cemented a change in American popular music in the 1920s.

Born in New Orleans, Louis made thousands of recordings, and most have been reissued and repackaged many times over the years. Keep in mind that Louis's recorded career stretched from 1923 until 1971. He was a master on the trumpet and arguably the most recognized figure playing the horn. He was a Grammy winner for his vocals in "Hello, Dolly!," and he earned the Grammy Lifetime Achievement Award in 1972. His iconic rendition of "When the Saints Go Marching In" became an American classic and is still used when the New Orleans Saints football team takes the field on game day.

TAKE IT

Fais Do Do ("fey doh doh") Cajun Dance—*several locations*
They say that nobody cooks like a Cajun, but have you heard how hot it gets on the dance floor? A Cajun dance party is referred to as a fais do do, and New Orleans offers several locations to learn how to move like the Boudreauxs, Landrys, Heberts, and the Terrebonnes who were taught how to dance in the bayous by their French-speaking grandparents. There's no doubting that the experience of dance lessons in an energizing and fun atmosphere will get you hooting and hollering to the two-step. With the French lyrics, you might even feel you're in another country. Mid City Lanes 'n' Bowl and Tropical Isle offer dance lessons, while other clubs play Cajun music.

Street musicians. *Courtesy of Zack Smith*

WHILE YOU'RE HERE

While in the Big Easy, walk **Magazine Street**, which features 6 miles of shopping in locally owned businesses offering jewelry, clothing, antiques, home décor, souvenirs, and so much more. What makes this strip even more special is the abundance of historic architecture with local color palettes and beautiful upscale homes. You'll encounter many tourists exploring the art galleries and the cafés, but the area is also as authentic as it gets, with locals going about their everyday lives. Take one of the city's famous streetcars to visit the nearby **Audubon Park** to check out local wildlife and exotic vegetation. A true treasure to the locals, this space opened in 1898 after hosting the World Cotton Centennial in 1884. You might find species you've never encountered elsewhere in this natural escape that showcases the beautiful oak trees, lagoons, and stunning wildlife. Named after artist and naturalist John James Audubon, a former resident of New Orleans, the park attracts locals and visitors alike for picnics, relaxing, special events, and taking advantage of the paved loop for walkers, joggers, cyclists, and rollerbladers.

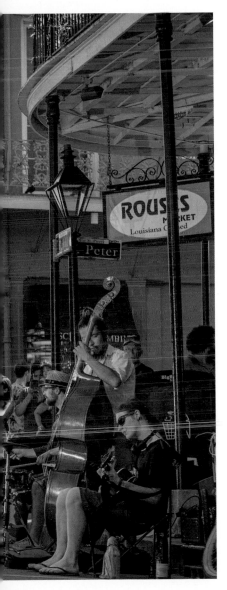

Best Jazz Clubs in New Orleans

It's not hard to find places to hear jazz in and around New Orleans, but Frenchmen Street is a great place to start. Here's a short list of venues suggested by locals. Pick a spot or two that best suits your curiosity and fits your schedule.

The Blue Nile—*532 Frenchmen Street*
One of the longest-standing clubs on Frenchmen Street, the Blue Nile in the city's Faubourg Marigny Historic District will make you want to stay out all night. The venue is the site of the first bar in the area to feature live music, and it remains an epicenter of the local music scene. Performers include some of the greatest musicians in the world in jazz, soul, funk, and even bluegrass; New Orleans legends Kermit Ruffins and Trombone Shorty and others often stop by to entertain audiences. With its blue lights

Royal Street buskers.
Courtesy of Zack Smith

inside the club, the Blue Nile really does live up to its name, and it offers an intimate setting where the audience is close to the stage. Music flows in and out of the doors, influencing listeners passing by in the streets. The scene is a perfect symbol of passion for music in New Orleans.

The Spotted Cat Music Club—*632 Frenchmen Street*
Just a little corner stage can make a giant impact. Two to three bands take that stage each night of the week at this Frenchman Street stop. It is an iconic venue for the city and the jazz genre, boosting its fame through features in television and films. This is quintessential New Orleans, and you'll feel like you're enjoying the jazz scene of the 1920s.

Fritzel's European Jazz Pub—*733 Bourbon Street*
Talk about sitting at the bar and being up close and personal! From local to international jazz musicians, the artists are nearly performing at your seat. Right in the French Quarter, Fritzel's attracts tourists but doesn't get the rowdy crowds, so if you're looking for an escape to enjoy traditional jazz without hearing the intoxicated flow of foot traffic, this is the venue. And, it's the oldest operating jazz club in the city for a reason.

Maple Leaf Bar—*8316 Oak Street*
Due its proximity to Tulane and Loyola University, don't be surprised to encounter a college crowd that makes this venue feel like an extended fraternity house. There's a quaint courtyard in the back as well as plenty of space in the front to hear performers such as James Booker, Papa Grows Funk, the Radiators, and the Rebirth Brass Band. A number of acts have recorded live albums on-site.

Tipitina's—*501 Napoleon Avenue*
One of the most notable music venues in New Orleans stands alone on Napoleon Avenue and Tchoupitoulas Street. In the uptown neighborhood, jazz, funk, soul, rock, R&B, reggae, and zydeco can be heard from the greatest talents around. There's a wall of fame on the side of the yellow building, featuring the Neville Brothers, Phish, Gigantic, and Professor Longhair, who named his song "Tipitina" after the club.

Frenchmen Street nightlife.
Courtesy of Zack Smith

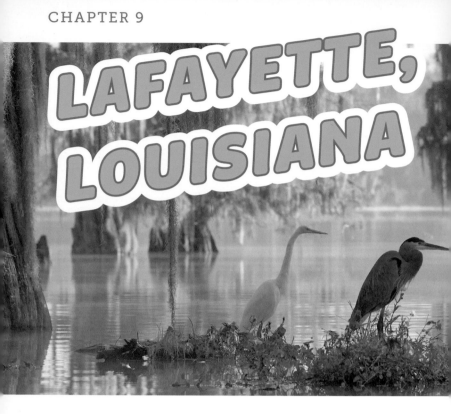

CHAPTER 9

LAFAYETTE, LOUISIANA

Right off Interstate 10, two hours from New Orleans, is Lafayette, Louisiana, which has been referred to as the Happiest City in America—and it's a distinction that makes sense when you factor in the combination of exquisite Cajun and Creole cuisine, deep roots of blended musical genres, colorful public-art pieces, and epic outdoor recreational opportunities among swamp creatures. Lafayette is the Heart of Acadiana, the official name given to the French Louisiana region. The city became home to

Acadian refugees who were expelled from Canada after Great Britain defeated France in the Seven Years' War. Their descendants became known as Cajuns, and you'll still notice the influence of the French language throughout the city today. Creole influences abound as well. As for the music, you may recognize that Cajun music is more jazz oriented and blues based, while Creole music has a more Caribbean and West African feel to it, but first let's learn more about who these two groups are.

🏨 CHECKING IN

Maison Mouton Plantation—
338 North Sterling Road
Soak into what life was like among the ancient oak trees on the plantation of the early 1800s. This restored Creole home turned into a bed-and-breakfast is the perfect way to experience southern charm with Old World furnishings used by the Acadians. Relax in the shaded courtyard or unwind on the front porch—this is the casual pace of the South.

💡 WHO ARE THE CAJUNS?

Hailing from the Vendee region of western France, the forebears of the Cajun people began settling in the New World in 1604, creating a home for themselves in Canada's Nova Scotia region, then known as Acadie. By 1713, the region was ruled by Great Britain, which began to deport the Acadians to other areas in 1755. Seeking a new home, some of the exiles made their way south to Louisiana and established settlements west of New Orleans.

According to the National Park Service, which administers the three Acadian cultural centers of Jean Lafitte National Historical Park and Preserve, "The new arrivals learned new skills and shared what they brought with them with the many peoples already in the area: American Indians, free people of color, enslaved Africans and their descendants, and immigrants from Europe, Asia, and North and South America. The Acadians became Cajuns as they adapted to their new home and its people." Over the years, the Cajuns' architecture, music, and food evolved to become entirely their own.

Lafayette art mural.
*Courtesy of
LafayetteTravel.com*

💡 WHO ARE THE CREOLES?

During the colonial days of Louisiana in the late 1700s, when French and Spanish settled the region, those who integrated with the African slaves were considered Creole. They also mixed with Native Americans, creating a unique blend of culture and genealogy pool. The language has diverged so much from its European roots that the Creole language is now identified as its own. In addition, as the demographic evolved, so did their music and food. Louisiana is home to over 300,000 Creoles, making for a rich history in this part of the world.

Cane River Creole National Historical Park's Oakland and Magnolia Plantations are excellent places to immerse oneself in the Creole culture and observe their past and continuing contributions to our entire nation.

Lafayette's sign invites visitors to stand in the center with their arms raised to form the Y. *Courtesy of LafayetteTravel.com*

⊙ WHILE YOU'RE HERE

Before getting deep into the music, take a visit to **Acadian Village**, a re-creation of a typical 1800s Cajun village. In order to educate visitors on the area's culture history, the design team transformed 10 acres of farmland into a shaded community with a bayou running through it. After you explore the village, the perfect way to view all the outdoor bounty of Lafayette and the surrounding areas is to take a swamp tour. Whether you opt for a high-speed air boat or a more leisurely paced boat, enjoy learning about the area from the boat's caption as you travel through the swamps and bayous and take in views of the cypress trees and alligators.

Acadian Village. *Courtesy of LafayetteTravel.com*

An airboat swamp tour. *Courtesy of LafayetteTravel.com*

A blue heron at Lake Martin. *Courtesy of LafayetteTravel.com*

A Musical Melting Pot

To say Lafayette is a melting pot is an understatement. The city has been a crossroads of cultures, bringing with them a wide range of music genres. Lafayette proudly boosts being home to more genres of music than just about anywhere. The French language combined with the traditional African songs created a percussive rhythm to stomp and clap, known as "la la" music. Newly introduced instruments, such as the accordion by the Germans, enhanced the spirit and vibrancy. Other instruments such as the fiddle intertwine with existing sounds, representing collaborative artistry to make beautiful music. Being considered

The triangle sculpture in Lafayette.
Courtesy of LafayetteTravel.com

the music of marshes, prairies, and muddy roads, Lafayette has accommodated all walks of lives to contribute to their identity. That way, the musical genres keep growing and sounds continue to be unique.

You can check out some of the local music at several zydeco clubs in town, which include **El Sid-O's Zydeco & Blues Club** at 1523 North St. Antoine Street and **Blue Moon Saloon & Guest House** at 215 East Convent Street. And after you've heard the rubboard and triangle instruments in action, Lafayette even offers you opportunities to craft musical instruments yourself.

MAKE IT

Lane Custom Metal—*101 Cesco Lane*
The T'fer or triangle is a symbol of the region. The instrument is so vital to the zydeco music that there is even a large sculpture of a triangle outside the Lafayette Visitors Center, which makes for a photo op that perfectly represents the area.

The instrument is simple yet iconic. It provides a rhythmic and percussive sound that was originally made by Acadian craftsmen with tines of rakes used for rice or hay. Get a chance to weld your own triangle by scheduling an appointment with Lane Custom Metal by calling 337-993-0475.

MAKE IT

Key of Z Rubboards—*385 Sandpiper Place, Sunset (15 miles north of Lafayette)*
All Key of Z rubboards are shaped and finished by hand, and there's a growing legacy behind each one. The first frottoir, also known as the rubboard, was used strictly as a musical instrument. The invention was born from that historical, chance encounter between Clifton Chenier, a now-famous Creole musician, and Willie Landry, a Cajun metal craftsman. To this day, Willie's son Tee Don Landry continues the valued tradition first established by his father in 1946. Make sure to call Tee Don at 337-654-0858 for an appointment to learn more about the crafting of this special instrument.

Tee Don Landry playing the rubboard. *Courtesy of Tee Don*

INTERVIEW WITH CRAFTSMAN TEE DON

What's the history behind your instrument?

My dad coinvented the rubboard with zydeco pioneer Clifton Chenier. He moved to Texas for a short period in the 1940s for metalwork and met Clifton in the refineries. Clifton's brother Cleveland played house dances using the old washboard with a rope. Clifton drew a design in the dirt at the worksite and asked my dad, "Can you make something like this?" He said sure. That's real craftsman ingenuity.

Years later, I took that ingenuity to create a business on making rubboards. I was always fascinated when Clifton played locally, and when I was in my thirties I checked out a documentary about him and noticed my dad's product in the film of old tin and steel.

Is it as easy to play as it looks?

People make fools of themselves when they come up on stage to try it. Of course, when they're drunk, it makes for a great show and a perfect time to use the restroom. It's hard to play with an instrument up against your body. It's like tapping your head and rubbing your tummy at the same time. People don't really think the rubboard is an instrument, instead a novelty. It's the attention-getter since many people haven't seen it used on stage, and that's why band leaders don't want it because it distracts attention away from them. I have made these for Kid Rock, Rihanna, and ZZ Top, to name a few.

CHAPTER 10

HOUSTON, TEXAS

A massive city, Houston represents everything big in Texas. Houston is the template for the future of America's cities. It has an alluring blend of diverse cultures, coexisting to redefine the checklist of urban amenities and features that are essential for prosperity and advancement. From the exuberant theater district and sport arenas to the

manicured greenspace, Houston aims to appeal to everyone, and that's why it's another major hub for music. And, the city's influence reaches across the state; from the gulf beaches in Galveston to the rodeo arenas and mariachi bands, Houston has it covered.

Fall foliage at Buffalo Bayou Park.
Courtesy of Visit Houston

The Whitehall—*1700 Smith Street* Downtown Houston is home to an original landmark hotel that speaks to everything elegant—from the grand lobby and ballrooms to the welcoming guest rooms and landscaped property. Built in 1963 with its midcentury architecture, the building enhances the city's skyline with its unique design. The Whitehall has a vision to entertain and dazzle its guests, and it's prepared to host large gatherings and create the ultimate Texas experience.

The Whitehall. *Courtesy of Visit Houston*

TAKE IT

Champion Forest Baptist Church—*15555 Stuebner Airline Road*
If Texas is home to megachurches, then that must mean the choirs
are big too. Houston is home to some of the world's largest
churches, and the gospel is sung throughout the city every Sunday.
As Yolanda Adams, one of the bestselling gospel artists of all
time, says, "There is a sound that comes from gospel music that
doesn't come from anywhere else. It is a sound of peace. It is a
sound of 'I'm going to make it through all of this.'"

Listening to the joyful music during a Sunday service, you
may wonder how much rehearsal goes into preparing for the

The Champion Forest choir. *Courtesy of
Champion Forest Baptist Church*

LARGEST CHURCHES IN HOUSTON

Texas is home to more than two hundred megachurches, and Houston has its share. According to Hartford Institute for Religion Research, here are the five largest churches in the city (ranked by attendance):

1. Lakewood Church—45,000
2. Woodlands Church—18,385
3. Second Baptist Church—15,970
4. New Light Christian Center Church—13,500
5. The Fountain of Praise—9,000

performance. Find out for yourself! Email the choir director of Champion Forest Baptist Church at music@cfbc.org to ask about participating in a rehearsal on a Wednesday evening. Singing with a choir is one of the most invigorating experiences, as you feel the power coming from a collection of harmonious voices.

Musical Theater

Taking advantage of Houston's **Theater District**, a highly concentrated center for the performing arts in downtown Houston, is a must. Like they say, everything is big in Texas—and so are the theaters. Find a show at the Hobby Center of Performing Arts, Broadway at the Hobby Center, Alley Theatre, Houston Grand Opera, Wortham Theatre Center, Houston Symphony at Jones Hall, or one of the other venues.

A performance of Mary Poppins lights up the Hobby Center.
Courtesy of Visit Houston

⊙ WHILE YOU'RE HERE

With Houston's more than 10,000 restaurants representing cuisine from more than seventy countries and American regions, the city's restaurant scene is as ethnically diverse as the more than six million residents in the Houston metro area. Indulge in a few local flavors while in the city—from barbecue to Tex-Mex and much, much more.

Houston food. *Courtesy of Visit Houston*

CHAPTER 11

This city didn't just happen; it was carefully planned by minds of compromising priorities. The active footpaths, sprightly sidewalks, vibrating venues, and serene blue space all are traits made to order in this gem of central Texas. Might as well bring a laptop to the trails, because Austin figured out how to make work into a playground. While the traditional culture of Texas tends to be serious,

Austin is an exception to the rule, flawlessly complementing work and play, drawing envy from all corners of the country. Ever hear of a low-star rating on Austin? Whether you're a visitor or a resident, Austin makes people happy. It's the nature within the city. It's the delicious food. It's the energy of the streets. It's the prestigious University of Texas. And, of course, it's the live music.

 # CHECKING IN

The Driskill Hotel—*604 Brazos Street* Every part of this property will be remembered for class and elegance, from the hallways to the balconies. The grand entrances, marble flooring, chandeliers, and prominent pillars are inviting. Located on the corner of Sixth Street and Brazos Street, this historic property illuminates the greatest Texas hospitality, since it's a place where hundreds gather for weddings, elegant dinners, and memorable stays. The entertainment on Sixth Street and the hotel compete for your attention, and you'll find it hard to check out, but there's lots to explore right outside the doors on Sixth Street.

The Driskill's lobby. *Courtesy of Visit Austin*

The Live Music Capital's Best Live Music Venues

Since Austin is the Live Music Capital of the World, you obviously can't visit without checking out some of its iconic music venues.

Broken Spoke—*3201 South Lamar Boulevard*
If you're looking for a dance hall that is guaranteed to be lively, this is it. They offer dance lessons on the Texas two-step every Wednesday through Saturday night. This place has been boot-scootin' since 1964 with stars such as Willie Nelson and Dolly Parton entertaining crowds.

Carousel Lounge—*1110 East 52nd Street*
Musical halls are so saturated in Austin, it's no wonder bars try to stand out from the crowd, and this colorful carnival-themed venue is no exception. With circus murals and an actual carousel on-site, visitors have been enjoying this place for all kinds of reasons besides music since 1963.

Continental Club & Gallery—*1315 South Congress Avenue*
Since its opening in 1955, it has been one of the oldest continuously running music clubs in Austin, and you can imagine all the history that has parked in front of that classic neon sign. You'll feel as if you've taken a step back in time as the tunes of rockabilly, country, rock, jazz, and soul rattles the walls. It's considered a swanky club, so don't let the retro look fool you.

ACL Live at the Moody Theater—*310 West Willie Nelson Blvd.*
Lines wrap around the block as formal concertgoers await a show in this state-of-the-art 2,750-person-capacity venue, which hosts around a hundred concerts per year. *Austin City*

Limits (ACL) is America's longest-running television music series, and its list of participating artists is so long that it has its own Wikipedia page. PBS features the long-standing series, which arguably has helped Austin earn its name as the Live Music Capital of the World. Make sure to take that selfie out front with the statue of Willie Nelson, the music legend with deep ties to Austin.

The Saxon Pub—*1320 South Lamar Boulevard*

Proudly boasting a live ticker of performances since 1990, this venue has welcomed over 30,000 musicians. The pub became such a staple of Austin that an airport location opened inside the terminal. At the original location, the frequency of shows is the main attraction, bringing in six acts in a single night.

Cactus Café—*2247 Guadalupe Street*

Located on the campus of the University of Texas, the Cactus Café showcases top international acts and several open-mic nights per week. Since its opening in 1979, the venue has helped launch the careers of a number of well-known musicians, including Lyle Lovett and Lucinda Williams.

HOW DID AUSTIN BECOME THE LIVE MUSIC CAPITAL OF THE WORLD?

According to the Austin Convention and Visitors Bureau, the city is home to more than 250 music venues ranging from small bars along Sixth Street to the Frank Erwin Center, located on the campus of the University of Texas at Austin, and Zilker Park. Multiple reports offer the simple explanation that Austin was dubbed the live music capital for having more live music venues per capita than anywhere else in the United States, but here's the slogan's real origin: an investigation by Mose Buchele, a correspondent for KUT 90.5, Austin's NPR station, led to the discovery that the earliest use of "Live Music Capital of the World" is found in an advertisement placed by the Austin Chamber of Commerce in the July 1985 issue of *Billboard* magazine. According to KUT 90.5, David Lord, who worked to promote Austin's music scene in the mid-'80s, says it was during a 1985 trip to a music industry conference in New York that the chamber decided to place the magazine ad and needed a slogan. According to Lord, the idea for the slogan came when someone in the group said, "I wonder how many places we can go see live music on a Monday night?" After looking at the concert listings in two Austin newspapers, the group tallied up more than seventy places and decided together that Austin is in fact the live music capital of the world.

Austin City Limits

Since 2002, Austin City Limits Music Festival has grown to attract nearly a half million music lovers on 300-plus acres in Zilker Park during the month of October. Spread over the course of two jammin' weekends, nine stages host more than 100 artists, including past performances by Guns N' Roses, Metallica, and Red Hot Chili Peppers. The festival was inspired by the original ACL Live music series, which has become its own attraction, even inspiring similar events in New Zealand and Australia.

Festival days. *Courtesy of Visit Austin*

MAKE IT

Song Confessional—*1101 Music Lane*

Want to connect with a local songwriter to custom-create a song based on your own life or idea? Through Song Confessional, people can visit a "confession booth" inside Hotel Magdalena and record a "confession" about their lives. Then, songwriters and musicians create a brand-new song based on the confession. KUTX radio in Austin plays these creations on the radio, with Walker Lukens and Zac Catanzaro hosting episodes that premiere songs that have been created based on people's stories, making this the greatest grassroots experience in music. The creation of a new song would be a great ending to an incredible trip through the South. Stop by the confession booth to record your memories of your journey through the music of the South, or you can share other stories about your life. Take as long you need, since the prompts explain the process step by step. The turnaround for a song could take several weeks.

Austin's Song Confessional.
Courtesy of Walker Lukens

A mural on Sixth Street. *Courtesy of Visit Austin*

Sixth Street

After recording your song confession, explore Sixth Street, which is one of the most bizarre and lively streets in the country—and one that is distinctly "Austin." With roughly 3 miles of a colorful and bustling array of bars, restaurants, and entertainment venues, it's a sure bet for experiencing local characters and the vibrancy of the city. Large televisions from the restaurants capture sports fans, outdoor patios capture the casual crowds, and the upbeat music captures the rest. The feel of Sixth Street changes block to block, from classy to grungy to sophisticated to college party. Check out the live music venues as you stroll the district.

If you're not ready to end your journey just yet, there's more musical heritage to explore in Texas. Head south to discover mariachi and much more.

Nearly half of Texas is Hispanic, and it would be a disservice not to include the Latin music influence within the state. About a five-hour drive south from Austin, the Rio Grande valley is right on the border between Mexico and the US, and it's a stone's throw away from the Gulf waters. A draw to the region is the distinct culture that knows how to party, or—as the locals say—*fiesta*. At the end of February and in early March, the city of Brownsville hosts Charro Days, which celebrates Mexican heritage from both sides of the border. If you're thinking that entails mariachi music, then you're right! Mariachi is highly cherished in the Rio Grande valley and is even offered as a major at local colleges, so those who graduate with a degree can teach the musical genre in Texas high schools. When you think high school and Texas, you're probably thinking football, and, indeed, many half-time shows at football games in Texas offer mariachi performances. Mariachi contains a small ensemble of various stringed instruments with an exchange of vocalists. They share the struggles, joy, and growth of people within the lyrics.

A few hours closer to Houston lies Corpus Christi, widely associated with the life and death of Selena, a mega Tejano musical star. Her hits from the 1990s and legacy still live on in Corpus Christi as the city grows its music scene. One event worth mentioning is the Dia de los Muertos Festival, which has become the city's largest event, honoring Mexico's national holiday that remembers and celebrates family members and friends lost. The costumes, floral headbands, and face painting are all part of the traditions that will be something to remember.

Most of the members in the Mariachi Margaritas group are music educators. *Courtesy of Mariachi Margaritas*

CHAPTER 12

THE END OF THE ROAD

America is defined by its music. America has defined music. It lives within our daily lives, creating emotional attachment to a joyful time or offering solace through a turbulent one. Musical artists create their masterpieces inspired by their own life experiences and the environment from which they came. Their voices resonate across the land, from the roads of blowing cotton to the wooden porches of the mountains, proving we all have similar emotions, though not needing to be identical. The human spirit is shared

through song, whether coming from Seattle-born grunge or Detroit's Motown or Los Angeles gangster rap and glam rock—but the Southern Region had an era of hysteria that generated a multitude of genres to forever be theirs and became the bedrock of America's music. Artists such as B.B. King, Louis Armstrong, Elvis Presley, Tina Turner, and Willie Nelson pioneered new sounds and styles and solidified this region's legacy, which will forever be cherished by new waves of musicians and musical fans.

There's no region in the world that has made more of a musical influence than the stretch of land from Lexington to Austin. It should be called the Music Belt. *Jammin' through the South* has taken you through these sacred lands of music, introducing you to Take It and Make It experiences that can enrich your travels. Crafting a fiddle in Kentucky and a guitar in Nashville will continue the legacy these destinations have worked tirelessly to create. Blowing through a harmonica in Mississippi and singing with a Houston choir exhibits an appreciation for local art. Tapping your feet at a New Orleans jazz club and standing in a crowded audience at an Austin concert validates the passion and love these artists carry. There's something about having been there and done that. After completing this journey, the next time you hear the lyrics of a musician from this region, they will resonate with you in a stronger, deeper way. The next time you see an instrument made in one of these states, you'll understand that these crafters are not only supplying a demand but also infusing their pride into it. Take what you've made and spread the word, as if you are a local.

ABOUT YOUR GUIDE

Daniel Seddiqui has been called the real-life Where's Waldo, and for good reason. He has traveled the entire US more than 20 times, earning recognition as "the Most Traveled Person in America." He sang with the Mormon Tabernacle Choir in Salt Lake City, shot archery with members of the Cherokee Nation, and built furniture with the Amish, among many dozens of other immersive experiences.

Daniel has been fueled by a lifelong love of maps, seeking meaningful connection, and fearlessly tackling societal challenges, eventually charting his own course to become a multitime international bestselling author, keynote speaker, career analyst, and travel entrepreneur. His work has been featured by many mainstream media outlets, including CNN, Fox News, *Psychology Today*, Time Inc., MSNBC, NPR, the *Today* show, *Newsweek*, *World News Tonight*, the *Wall Street Journal*, and *USA Today*. He lives in Bend, Oregon.

For more information on Daniel, including details on the organized tours he leads for those interested in traveling with a group, visit www.livingthemap.com.

JANET DAILEY

CALDER BORN, CALDER BRED

POCKET BOOKS

New York   London   Toronto   Sydney   Singapore

This book is a work of historical fiction. Names, characters, places, and incidents relating to nonhistorical figures are products of the author's imagination or are used fictitiously. Any resemblance of such nonhistorical incidents, places, or figures to actual events or locales or persons living or dead is entirely coincidental.

An *Original* Publication of POCKET BOOKS

POCKET BOOKS, a division of Simon & Schuster, Inc.
1230 Avenue of the Americas, New York, NY 10020

Copyright © 1983 by Janet Dailey

ISBN: 0-671-04049-9

First Pocket Books mass market printing April 1984

23 22 21 20 19 18

POCKET and colophon are registered trademarks of Simon & Schuster Inc.

Cover photo by Ric Ergenbright
Cover design by Jim Lebbad

Printed in the U.S.A.